CD INCLUDED

TENOR SAXOPHONE

HAL•LEONARD
BIG BAND
PLAY-ALONG
VOLUME 2

Popular Hits

T0039908

ISBN-13: 978-1-4234-2228-0
ISBN-10: 1-4234-2228-7

HAL•LEONARD®
CORPORATION
7777 W. BLUEMOUND RD. P.O. BOX 13819 MILWAUKEE, WI 53213

Visit Hal Leonard Online at
www.halleonard.com

Popular Hits

AIN'T NO MOUNTAIN HIGH ENOUGH

TENOR SAX

Words and Music by
NICKOLAS ASHFORD and VALERIE SIMPSON
Arranged by ROGER HOLMES

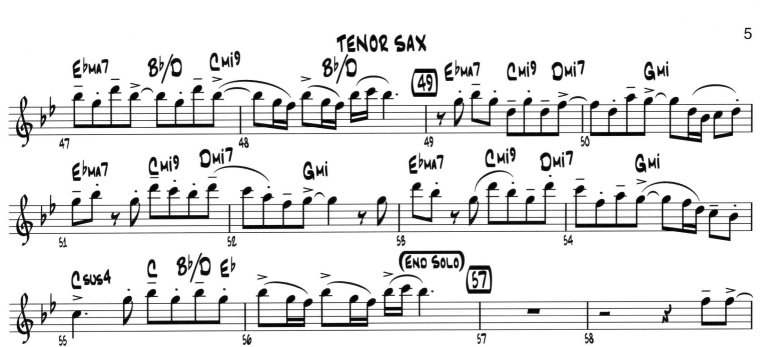

BRICK HOUSE

TENOR SAX

Words and Music by LIONEL RICHIE, RONALD LaPREAD,
WALTER ORANGE, MILAN WILLIAMS,
THOMAS McCLARY and WILLIAM KING

Arranged by PAUL MURTHA

TENOR SAX

Play 3 times – tacet 1st time

COPACABANA
(At The Copa)

Words by BRUCE SUSSMAN and JACK FELDMAN
Music by BARRY MANILOW
Arranged by JOHN BERRY

Tenor Sax

TENOR SAX

Recorded by SANTANA
EVIL WAYS

TENOR SAX

Words and Music by SONNY HENRY
Arranged by ROGER HOLMES

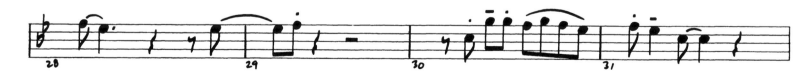

TENOR SAX

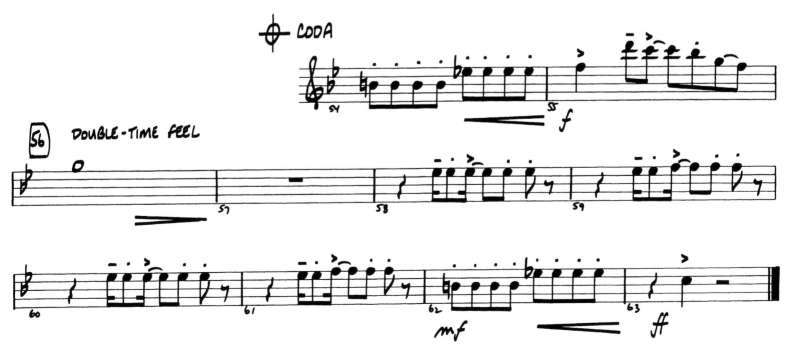

I HEARD IT THROUGH THE GRAPEVINE

Tenor Sax

Words and Music by
NORMAN J. WHITFIELD and BARRETT STRONG
Arranged by JOHN BERRY

TENOR SAX

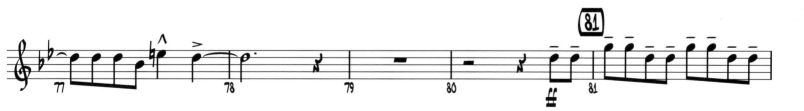

Recorded by GEORGE BENSON

on broadway

Words and Music by
**BARRY MANN, CYNTHIA WEIL,
MIKE STOLLER and JERRY LEIBER**
Arranged by JOHN HIGGINS

TENOR SAX

TENOR SAX

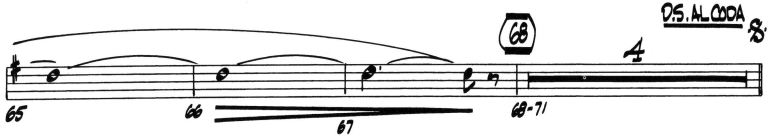

Recorded by ARETHA FRANKLIN
RESPECT

Words and Music by
OTIS REDDING
Arranged by PAUL MURTHA

TENOR SAX

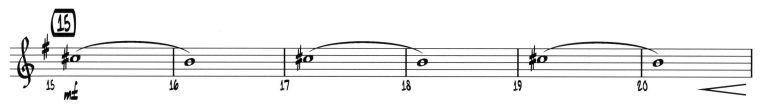

TENOR SAX

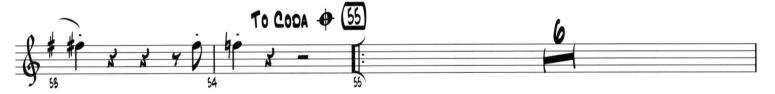

STREET LIFE

Tenor Sax

Words and Music by
WILL JENNINGS and JOE SAMPLE
Arranged by RICK STITZEL

(Medium Funk)

TENOR SAX

YESTERDAY

Tenor Sax

Words and Music by
JOHN LENNON and PAUL McCARTNEY
Arranged by JOHN BERRY

TENOR SAX

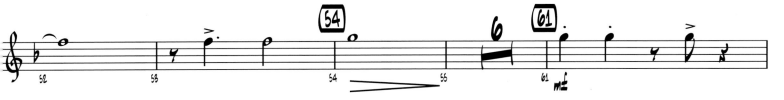

Recorded by THE CHERRY POPPIN' DADDIES

ZOOT SUIT RIOT

TENOR SAX

Words and Music by STEVE PERRY
Arranged by PAUL MURTHA

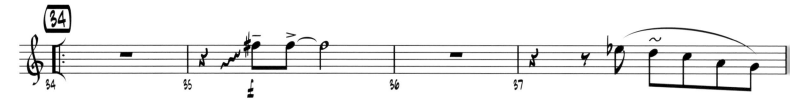

TENOR SAX